CW00853429

Woodworking

The Complete Woodworking Tips and Starting Simple Projects for Beginners

Copyright © 2020

All rights reserved.

DEDICATION

The author and publisher have provided this e-book to you for your personal use only. You may not make this e-book publicly available in any way. Copyright infringement is against the law. If you believe the copy of this e-book you are reading infringes on the author's copyright, please notify the publisher at: https://us.macmillan.com/piracy

Contents

Woodworking Tips

Tips for Choosing the Perfect Wood

There are many reasons why people are into woodworking. It's a good hobby if you want to develop mindfulness. You must focus if you don't want to ruin the project you're working on or worse, injure yourself.

Woodworking can also be as simple or as technical as you want. You can experiment with tools, techniques, finishes, and so on. There's something for everyone, regardless of skill level.

Whatever your reason is for taking up woodworking, you can't forget about the basics. Here we'll talk about some tips on choosing the best wood for your furniture project.

1. Don't Shy Away from Softer Woods

Of course, you want the most durable wood for your furniture project. However, if you're a beginner or if you're looking to save some money, it's okay to go for softwoods, such as pine, cedar, fir, and redwood.

Also, if you're working on a workbench, for example, you can use a mix of hardwood and softwood. The base can be pine, while the tops and the vice could be maple or beech. You can choose hardwood for parts that need to be durable and go for a softer wood for those areas that won't take a beating.

2. Know the Effect of Humidity on Wood Stability

Did you know that increased humidity makes wood expand in width? You must consider this when choosing wood for a wooden door.

While it's okay to use a less stable wood for the panels, you have to go for a more stable option (i.e., wood with stable vertical grain) for the rails and stiles. Tip: It's easier to choose if you understand how wood is milled from the tree.

3. Check for Wood Defects

Just because durability is your number one priority doesn't mean you should forget wood defects, such as knots, insect holes, sapwood, and so on. When choosing wood for your furniture project, also consider how easy it's to work with.

If you don't use power tools, this is even more important. Working with hand tools is already tough. Don't make it harder on yourself by having to deal with bowed boards or wood that cups or twists.

4. Consider Exotic Woods

When used in flooring, exotic woods give off a contemporary look. Also, compared to domestic hardwoods, exotic woods are harder and denser.

If you want your furniture project to exude a modern vibe, exotic species, such as Brazilian Walnut, Australian Cypress, and Purpleheart, are good options.

5. Buy from Trusted Wood Providers

Can't find what you're looking for in your local hardware store? Try to expand your search to mills and dealers whose specialty is

To eliminate stains caused by oozing glue along joints, clamp the pieces together without glue. Apply masking tape over the joint and then cut it with a utility knife.

Next, separate the pieces, apply the glue, and clamp them together again. The glue will ooze onto the tape, not the wood. Remove the tape before the glue dries.

5 – Measure with a drafting square

Make accurate measuring and marking layouts on boards faster and easier with a drafting square – available at any art supply store.

When you need an accurate square in the 2- to 3-foot range, drafting squares beat the cumbersome drywall squares for accuracy and eliminate the hassle of hooking up a carpenter square.

6 – Keep a clean, orderly workspace

Achieving efficiency in your shop can sometimes be as simple as clearing clutter from your work area. A disorderly work area can hinder your productivity.

Another tip: Only keep out items that you use daily. Everything else should be put in designated areas so they're quickly retrievable when needed.

7 – Keep a well-lit shop

Pay special attention to lighting. You should have consistent and ample illumination on all work areas so you can work from any angle without casting shadows. This ensures safety and productivity.

Consider:

Overhead lighting

Focused lighting

On-tool lights

Painting walls and the ceiling white can help diffuse the light.

8 – Keep your blades sharp

Dull tools such as chisels, blades, planes, scrapers and gouges don't cut cleanly. They tear at the wood fibers resulting in a fuzzy, uneven, unprofessional look.

Tools that have been chipped or nicked require grinding. A bench grinder, wet grinder, or even a belt sander can be used.

Avoid letting your tool get too hot when using a bench grinder or belt sander to prevent it from losing temper. Dipping it in a pan of cool water every few seconds will help.

After grinding, proceed to honing using either a flat wet stone or oil stone. A wet stone is preferred when doing fine woodworking.

Clamp Small Stuff With Hot Glue

1. Hot glue holds small stuff better than clamps

When you have to cut, shape, file, sand or finish something small, reach for your hot glue gun and glue the piece to a pedestal stick. The hot glue will hold just about anything as well as or better than any clamp ever could—if using a clamp is even possible. When your project is complete, try to pop it loose with a putty knife, but don't use too much force—you might tear out the wood or break the piece.

2. Try cold or heat to un-stick it

You have two options for breaking the grip: cold and heat. First, try sticking the work piece into the freezer for an hour or so. Frozen glue will usually give way with very little force. If that doesn't work, try a hair dryer to soften the glue. Still stuck? Reach for the heat gun. But warm the piece slowly and from a distance to avoid scorching the wood or damaging the finish.

Stair Gauge Cutting Guide

1. Use stair gauges as a crosscut guide

Stair gauges are usually used to lay out stair jacks. You clamp them to a carpenter's square to match the rise and run of a stair jack and then mark the notches. But if you put them both on the same tongue of a carpenter's square, the combination makes a great crosscut guide for circular saws.

2. Versatile and inexpensive

Pick up a pair for less than $5 at any hardware store or home center. Clamp the square in place so it won't slide around while you're cutting. You wouldn't like that one bit.

Invest In A Great Backsaw

Backsaws are a must for cutting joinery and other fine woodworking, but with so many sizes and tooth configurations available, it can be difficult to sort them out and more so to choose one saw that can perform a wide variety of tasks. Yet that is just what this short article will do for you right here.

Meet the family

A backsaw consists of a long rectangular blade (saw plate), a wooden handle, and most important, a thick metal back that is folded over the top of the blade. The back stiffens and straightens the blade so it can cut accurately, and adds weight and balance.

Backsaws come in a range of blade lengths with proportionate blade depths and plate thicknesses. Smallest are dovetail saws with blades 8 - 10" long. Carcase saws are about 12" long, sash saws 14", and tenon saws 14 - 16". But the best way to understand the family of backsaws is to put the names aside and instead think of function. For this, consider the two broad area of woodworking: case joinery, particularly dovetails, and post and rail joinery, which is mostly mortise and tenon joinery with its many variations.

A full set of saws

Sawing dovetails involves relatively small but very precise rip cuts. For this work, a backsaw about 10" long with about 15 rip teeth per inch will perform well. A typical plate thickness for such a saw is .018" with about 2" of blade depth under the back.

Sawing tenon cheeks requires a much more robust rip cut so a bigger saw is in order: 14" long (16" for larger work) with a .025" saw plate with 11 - 12 rip teeth per inch, and about 3 1/2" of depth.

In addition to these rips cuts, there are all sorts of crosscutting tasks such as tenon shoulders, miters, dados, and various trimmings. A 12" long saw, with a .020" plate filed with about 14 crosscut teeth per inch will handle this work.

Thus, a set of three or four saws would be considered ideal to manage almost all joinery work. My set of saws, shown in the photo, consists of, from top to bottom, a 16" rip for large tenons, 14" rip for most tenons and general joinery rip cuts, a 12" saw that I'll discuss more below, and a 10" rip for dovetailing.

Take a closer look

A slight modification to the teeth of the mid-size 12" saw can make it much more versatile. The key is in the tooth design.

A detailed discussed of tooth design is beyond the scope of this article but think of rip teeth as basically a row of tiny chisels with their edges at 90° to length of the row. These plow a kerf along the grain of the wood. Crosscut teeth are like tiny V-point knives arranged alternately with the bevels facing the midline of the row. These sever the wood fibers to create a kerf across the grain.

The saw filer creates rip teeth by pushing the file perpendicular to length of the saw. For crosscut teeth the file is oriented about 25° away from this to create bevels on the inside faces of the teeth.

But how about somewhere in between, where the file is angled say 15° or so? Well then we create a tooth line that is capable of good ripping and good crosscutting. In fact, my 12" saw has such "hybrid" teeth, as described and made by master saw wright, Mark Harrell of Bad Axe Tool Works, and I work just fine without a dedicated crosscut saw, even for fine work. The close up photos below show front and side views of the tooth line.

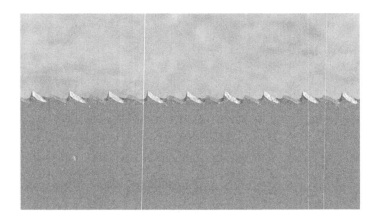

Conclusion

That 12" saw is a great choice for your first backsaw and will even perform quite well as your only backsaw. Sharpened with "hybrid" teeth, as described above, it will rip surprisingly well for dovetailing, crosscut remarkably cleanly, and has enough plate depth at 2 3/8" for sawing small to medium tenon cheeks.

Later, you probably will want to acquire dedicated backsaws for a full set. However, even with a set of three or four saws, your mid-size first saw will not be obsolete or underutilized at all. It will be your go-to saw for joinery crosscuts and will probably see more use for general bench work than any of the other saws. If, for some reason, you prefer a dedicated crosscut-tooth saw, it can always be re-filed as such.

Beginner Woodworking Projects

Make a Wooden Chopping Board and Serving Tray

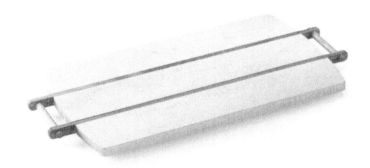

Looking for a satisfying woodworking project? Make this beautiful maple and walnut cutting board/serving tray. Simple enough that you can start in the morning, then finish it in the afternoon.

TIME: One day

COMPLEXITY: Simple

COST: Under $20

Before you start making a wood cutting board, we'll show you a simple way to dry-fit the parts, scribe the arc and then glue the whole works together. We used a 4-ft. steel ruler to scribe the arcs, but a yardstick or any thin board would also work. Be sure to use water-resistant wood glue and keep your tray out of the dishwasher or it might fall apart. And one more thing: Keep the boards as even as possible during glue-up to minimize sanding later.

Step-by-step

1. Mark the curves

Drill 1/2-in. holes centered 3/4 in. in from the ends of the walnut strips. Then lightly clamp all five boards together so you can scribe the arcs on the ends.

2. Assemble

Take the boards out of the clamp, saw and sand the arcs on each board, and then glue the assembly together, leaving the dowel handles unglued.

3. Finish up

Unclamp, sand both sides and drill a 1/4-in.-deep, 3/4-in.-diameter hole at each underside corner. Glue in the feet and dowel handles, then wipe on a couple of coats of Butcher Block Oil. That's it—chop some veggies!

Required Tools for this Project

Have the necessary tools for this DIY project lined up before you start—you'll save time and frustration.

Cordless drill

Forstner drill bits

Jigsaw

Miter saw

Orbital sander

Safety glasses

Tape measure

Required Materials for this Project

Avoid last-minute shopping trips by having all your materials ready ahead of time. Here's a list.

Four 3/4-in. x 3/4-in.-diameter dowels (for feet)

Three 20-in. x 3-1/2-in. maple boards

Two 23-1/2-in. x 1/2-in. x 3/4-in. walnut strips (handle strips)

Two 5-in. x 1/2-in.-diameter dowels (handles)

Build a Shoe Organizer

Store shoes up off the floor in clean, natural wood racks. This simple storage rack can handle everything from winter boots to summer sandals, with no mud buildup or scuff marks on the wall.

TIME: Instant!

COMPLEXITY: Super Simple!

COST: Under $20

Step-by-step

1. Clamp the 1×3 support to a piece of scrap wood as you drill

the holes to prevent the wood from splintering.

2. Screw the pieces together

3. Predrill through the back of the 1×4 into the 1×3 supports, then glue and screw the pieces together.

Required Tools for this build a shoe rack project

Have the necessary tools for this DIY project lined up before you start—you'll save time and frustration.

4-in-1 screwdriver

Clamps

Cordless drill

Countersink drill bit

Level

Miter saw

Tape measure

Required Materials for this build a shoe rack project

Avoid last-minute shopping trips by having all your materials ready ahead of time. Here's a list.

1-5/8-in. screws

1. Mark the cuts

To begin building these wooden storage containers, first cut the 1/4-in. plywood into eight 11-1/2-in. x 11-in. pieces. Use a 5-gallon bucket to trace a graceful S-curve from the 11-1/2-in.-high corner across the plywood to a 6-in. mark on the opposite side. Simply establish a smooth curve.

2. Cut the curves

Stack pairs so the best sides face each other and tape all the sheets together flush at the edges. "Gang cut" the curve with a jigsaw or a band saw.

3. Nail the pieces

Saw pine boards into 6-, 9-1/2- and 11-1/2-in. lengths. Drill 1-in.-diameter finger pulls in the 6-in. pieces, then nail the frames together. Nail the sides to the frames with 1-in. finish nails, sand as needed and apply a finish.

Required Tools for this Project

Have the necessary tools for this DIY project lined up before you start—you'll save time and frustration.

Air compressor

Air hose

Brad nail gun

Circular saw

Cordless drill

Drill bit set

Jigsaw

Orbital sander

Safety glasses

You'll also need a 5-gallon bucket.

Required Materials for this Project

Avoid last-minute shopping trips by having all your materials ready ahead of time. Here's a list.

1 x 4 pine

1/4-in. Plywood

Create a Sleek and Simple Coat and Hat Rack

Step-by-step

1. Position the racks

Drive your screws partway into each board so the screw tips poke out the back. Place the boards where you want them, and press hard to mark the spots for your drywall anchors.

2. Install drywall anchors

Screw your anchors into each marked spot and then attach the boards.

3. Drywall anchors

These anchors are quick and easy to install.

Organize your hallway or mudroom with this simple, attractive coat and hat rack. You just cut the boards to fit your space, paint them, outfit them with different kinds of hooks to suit your needs and then screw them to the wall. We used 6-ft.-long 1x4s, but use whatever length works for you and the space available. We chose poplar, which is the best choice if you want a painted finish. If you're after a natural wood look, choose any species you want.

Finish the boards first and then attach your hooks. We used drawer pulls down the middle and a robe hook near the top to hold backpacks and larger items. You'll find hooks in a tremendous range of styles, colors and prices at hardware stores and online retailers.

Attach the boards to studs, or to the drywall with screw-in drywall anchors (E-Z Ancor is one brand). Drive three screws in each board: one at the top, one in the middle and one at the bottom. Now you have a great place to hang your hat.

Required Tools for this coat and hat rack project

Have the necessary tools for this DIY project lined up before you start—you'll save time and frustration.

4-in-1 screwdriver

Circular saw

Level

Paintbrush

Required Materials for this coat and hat rack project

Avoid last-minute shopping trips by having all your materials ready ahead of time. Here's a list.

1x4 board

Drywall anchors

Hooks

Paint

Primer

Sandpaper

Two-Tier Drawer Spice Rack

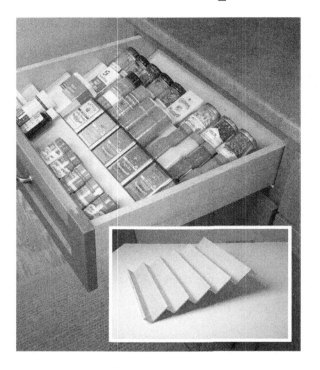

This spice rack drawer is not only a space-saver but also a smart organizer since all the spices are in one place, face up. We used the same basic design to make a two-tier utensil drawer too.

TIME: One day

COMPLEXITY: Moderate

COST: $20 – $100

Step-by-step

1. Cut away the top half of the drawer back

Use a jigsaw to cut away a little more than half of the drawer back.

2. Install the tray slides

Secure full-extension drawer slides to the top inside edges of the drawer. Install them "backward" so they extend toward the back of the drawer. It's OK if they run an inch or so beyond the back of the drawer; most cabinets have extra space in back.

3. Build the upper tray

Since most standard drawer glides are 1/2 in. wide, build your tray 1 in. narrower (or a hair less) than the inside width of the drawer. Build your tray the same length as the inside drawer length. Install partitions according to your needs.

4. Install the tray

Attach the plywood bottom to the tray with nails or brads. Screw the tray to the drawer slides so the top of the tray is flush with the top of the drawer. Then reinstall the drawer.

Recently we remodeled our kitchen: new cabinets, countertops, appliances, the works. Yet the first thing we show off when people visit isn't the fancy new stove, but the $20 two-tier spice tray. When we open the drawer, we can slide the top tray all the way back into the cabinet to access the entire bottom layer; no need to lift out a separate tray or sort through layers of stuff.

Do a little measuring before diving into this project. You can install the 1-3/4-in.-thick tray (like ours) if your drawer is at least 4 in. deep on the inside. Also, these trays are most useful if your existing drawers have (or you install) fullextension slides on the main drawer.

Required Tools for this Project

Have the necessary tools for this DIY project lined up before you start—you'll save time and frustration.

Air compressor

Air hose

Brad nail gun

Cordless drill

Jigsaw

Miter saw

Required Materials for this Project

Avoid last-minute shopping trips by having all your materials ready ahead of time. Here's a list.

2' x 4' 1/2" Plywood

Brad nails

Drawer slides

Build a Rustic Tree Branch Shelf

Need a quick, distinctive display shelf? Make this tree branch shelf from all-natural materials. Just cut the supports from branches, screw on a shelf, attach it to the wall and you're done!

TIME: Instant!

COMPLEXITY: Super Simple!

COST: Under $20

Step-by-step

1. Cut the branches

Build a simple jig to hold the branch steady. Cut the ends flush with the end of the jig.

2. Drill shelf holes

Trace around the branches where they touch the shelf bottom, then drill the holes and screw the shelf to the branches.

3. Fasten the tree branch shelf to the wall

Drill pilot holes near the top and bottom of the branch into the drywall. Then sink drywall anchors and screw the shelf to the wall.

Bring a bit of nature indoors with this simple branch-supported tree branch shelf. You'll have to find two forked branches about 1 in. in diameter, with one relatively straight side that will sit as flush to the wall as possible. We trimmed our branches from a crab apple, but you can use any smooth-barked tree. Our tree branch shelf is 12-in. melamine closet shelving with the ends painted white. Yours can be any wood you like, but keep the width to 12 in. or less.

To make square cuts on the branch ends, create a jig with scrap wood and a 2×4. Clamp the jig to your workbench. Then clamp each branch to the 2×4 and use the bottom edge of the jig to guide your cuts (Photo 1). Cut the branches above the crotch where the ends will be wide enough to support the shelf—one near the wall, the other close to the edge.

Clamp the tree branch shelf to the jig and trace around the branch. Drill pilot holes near the bottom of the marks at the front edge of the shelf so the screw tips won't poke through the branch (Photo 2). Bore countersink holes for the screw heads at the top of the shelf. Then hold the branches tight to the shelf while screwing them in. Hold the shelf level while you drill two holes through each branch into the drywall to mark the wall for drywall anchors. Screw your new tree branch shelf to the wall and fill it with your treasures.

Required Tools for this Project

Have the necessary tools for this DIY project lined up before you start—you'll save time and frustration.

4-in-1 screwdriver

Clamps

Cordless drill

Drill bit set

Handsaw

Level

Stepladder

Stud finder

Tape measure

Required Materials for this Project

Avoid last-minute shopping trips by having all your materials ready ahead of time. Here's a list.

1x12 shelf

24 x 48 x 3/4-in. plywood

2x4

Branches

Drywall anchors

Screws

Simple Step Stool

Here's a great gift idea that will draw raves. The joints are accurately made in seconds with a plate jointer, but don't tell your admirers. You'll also need a power saw to crosscut the boards and a jigsaw to cut the half-circles in the risers. The lumber you'll need:

One 8-ft. 1×8 clear hardwood board (actual width is 7-1/4 in. and actual thickness is 3/4 in.). Oak is a good choice because it's readily available at home centers.

One 4-ft. 1×3 hardwood board (actual width is 2-1/2 in. and actual thickness is 3/4 in.).

Cut the 8-ft. board into:

Two 22-in. riser boards

Two 11-in. riser boards

One 14-in. step board

One 14-in. seat board

You'll use 94 in. of the 96-in. board, so make practice cuts on a scrap board first to check the angle and length of cut. Don't cut the 3-ft. 1×3 board until you've dry-assembled the step, seat and risers and measured for a perfect fit.

To create two risers, join the 11-in. boards to the 22-in. boards with No. 20 biscuits and glue. Let dry 30 minutes, then lay the step and seat across and mark for two No. 20 biscuits at each joint. Dry-assemble the step, seat and risers with biscuits, then cut and snugly fit the crosspieces. Mark the riser-to-crosspiece joint and cut slots for No. 0 biscuits. Glue and firmly clamp the step, seat and crosspieces to the risers. Check for square and let dry 30 minutes, then cut out the 4-1/2 in. diameter arc on the bottom of the risers to create the legs. Finish-sand and apply your favorite finish. This project is designed for use on hard-surface flooring only – not carpeting.

Make a Swedish Boot Scraper

Build this handy boot scraper yourself in less than two hours. Now you can clean your muddy boots hands-free and help keep your entryway clean. Works great on snow clogged boots as well.

TIME: One day

COMPLEXITY: Simple

COST: $20 – $100

Build the boot scraper

Ordinary doormats simply can't handle serious muck, but you can clean out packed dirt from even the deepest boot treads with this boot scraper made from 2x4s.

Screw the base pieces (A and B) together upside down so that the screw heads are hidden.

Fasten the uprights (C) to the sides (D), then screw the side brushes on with 2-in. screws.

Screw the bottom brushes to the base with 2-in. screws.

Space the side pieces so that the bristles are roughly 4-1/2 in. apart.

Add a piece of aluminum angle to the front edge so you can scrape boots before brushing them.

Use stiff-bristle brushes—either "bilevel" brushes or deck scrub brushes. You may need to cut off part of the handle so the brush will lie flat.

Required Tools for this Project

Have the necessary tools for this DIY project lined up before you start—you'll save time and frustration.

Circular saw

Combination square

Drill/driver - cordless

Hacksaw

Miter saw

Tape measure

Required Materials for this Project

Avoid last-minute shopping trips by having all your materials ready ahead of time. Here's a list.

10" of aluminum angle (any size)

2-1/2-in. deck screws

2-in. deck screws

Four stiff-bristle brushes (bilevel or regular deck scrub brush)

Three 8-ft. 2x4s

Double Decker Garage Storage Shelves

Introduction

Floor space in most garages is hard to come by so the best place to find storage space for garage shelves is overhead. You can make your own DIY shelves for the garage easily go double-decker for twice the storage capacity.

Family Handyman

Tools Required

Circular saw

Cordless drill

Table saw

Materials Required

1-5/8-in. screws

Lag screws

Plywood: 1x2

Plywood: 1x3

Plywood: 1x8

Plywood: 2x8

Build the Shelves

This project has a 16-in. top shelf for big items, a 5-in. lower shelf and plenty of hook space. Need different size shelves or more space between them? It's easy to modify this basic design. To build a saw guide like ours, learn how to create circular saw cutting guides for plywood.

Step-by-step

1. Rip the Plywood Top to Width

Use a homemade saw guide and a circular saw, or a table saw, to cut the plywood for the 16-in.-wide top shelf.

2. Screw the Framework Together

Use all-purpose screws (4 inch lag screws and 1-5/8 inch screws) to secure the 1x8 back rim and 1x2 front rim to the 2x8 support block. Space the support blocks every 32 in.

3. Complete Assembling the Shelf

Install the plywood top, bottom shelf and the 1×2 and 1×3 lips. Use construction adhesive for added strength.

4. Secure the Shelf to the Wall

Use 4-in. lag or construction screws to secure the 1x8 back rim to the wall studs. Drive two screws into each stud—one high, one low.

5. Garage Shelf Dimensions

This shelf is 8 ft. long, but yours can be any length.

Organizing a garage isn't a one-size-fits-all project, so we've compiled some of our best garage storage ideas. Check out these 50 tips to find ways to make your garage more organized and better to use.

Printed in Great Britain
by Amazon

15266859R00038